Be: Common Sense for Uncommon People

Copyright © 2018 by Gabriel Soler
All rights reserved. This book or any portion thereof
may not be reproduced or used in any manner whatsoever
without the express written permission of the publisher
except for the use of brief quotations in a book review.

ISBN 13: 9781983049460

Amazon.com KDP Publishing
Amazon.com Kindle Direct Publishing

Navigation

Intro	1
A. The Truth & representation of the truth	6
B. Forever smaller perspective and forever larger perspective	12
C. Direction and focus with positive steps	17
D. Achieving a Goal	26
E. Understanding Obstacles	31
F. Win-Win	47
G. Win-Win now, Win-Win later	52
Conclusion	61
Additional Resources	63

Intro

THERE ARE BIG ideas that should be represented, expressed, and understood, before more complex and detailed ideas are expressed. Big ideas are generally agreed-on decisions most people would agree to. Complex and detailed ideas are very specific examples describing specific behavior that aren't always 100% agreed on and might have exceptions, gray areas, or overlaps with different types of behavior.

Life sometimes can be overwhelming. There are many different ideas, thoughts, people, places, customs, social norms, and varying responsibilities that are expected of different people, at different times, in different places.

Figuring out what is expected of you to reach a goal can be difficult if not absolutely impossible at times. But like the great Tracy Jordan (from the TV show "30 Rock") said,

"Nothing's impossible in life, except for dinosaurs". It gets confusing sometimes, like that quote, however it gets easier. Let's start big.

People are physical
People are born. We all know this already. However, there is the physical body of the person that is born and then the mind and spirit behind this person. The mind and spirit is what we are made up of. This is how we process information, value one feeling over another. This is who we really are. We get bodies that we carry around, each one is slightly different than another. But what we do with these bodies is what our mind and spirit want it to do.

Our bodies at the same time, give us feedback on our physical environment. It tells us if we are hungry, hot, tired, full, cold, or energized. Our body provides sensations and feelings that our own internal, mind and spirit process. There is our body accepting information and sensations the environment around us gives us, our mind-spirit processing information and sensations our body gives us, and our body listening to things our mind-spirit tell our bodies to do in the environment- giving sensations and molding the environment around us. We are born into a sort of see-saw- where there is a constant back and forth between our environment, our bodies, and our mind-spirit.

Between these three, the environment produces physical-sensations we have by coming into contact with our body, our body relays information about what sensations the outside environment is causing to our mind-spirit, and our mind-spirit determines what to do with this information.

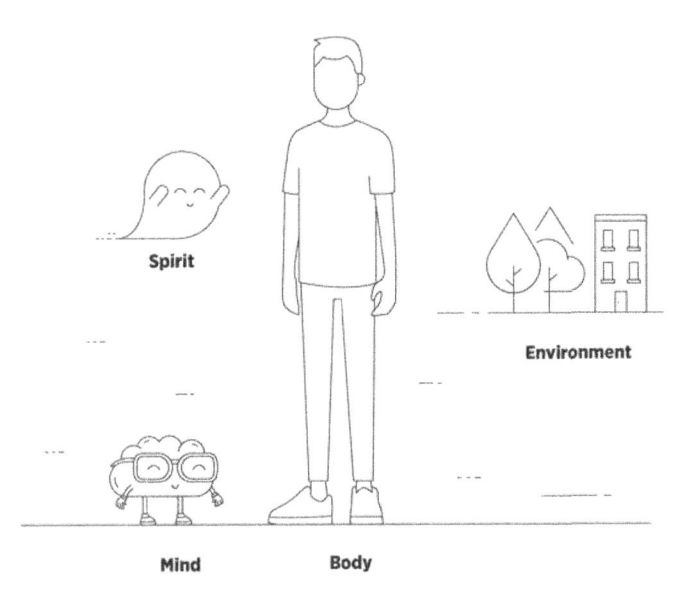

This is the basis of human conditioning. Since birth whether you have been aware of it or not, you've been conditioned through the environment. This can be as simple as getting caught in the rain, so now when it rains outside you expect to get wet. Touching a hot stove has taught you to be careful of heated objects. Sipping water while thirsty has taught you to feel refreshed afterwards. This is common, this happened to all of us, it's just the type of conditioning that we each have been through is slightly different. Our body might tell our mind-spirit we're getting wet and our mind-spirit might respond "this is wet. this bit of wetness feels good" and decide to keep on walking. Or "this is wet. this bit of wetness does not feel good", and decide to avoid the rain. These small differences in how we feel about the same environment is no better or worse- just how we decide to react to the same environment could be different.

Each small difference in our we react to our environment adds to support we can give to others, or support we would appreciate from others. If you're the type of person that doesn't mind walking in the rain, however your companion does, you can offer support to your companion by walking in the rain and letting them avoid it (you could walk in the rain to accomplish something, and let them stay dry). This is a way you can offer support to another person. Or the opposite. Your companion may prefer to walk in the rain, while you prefer being dry- so while being dry, you could accomplish tasks being dry while your companion gets wet. Each person has a strength, and a weakness. Each person has a preference of what they would like to do, and what they would not like to do.

The person you are, and the personality you have is a combination of your body-mind-spirit. The way you feel about certain things in the environment is the cause of conditioning. The everyday experience of your life has conditioned you and helped to make you into the person you are today.

The environment influences your body, but with your mind-spirit being a guide for your body, you've decided how to react to that environment. Over time, you have developed a set of beliefs in you that gives you decision-making-ability over your environment and over your feelings. You feel if something is good or bad, and want more or less of something because of how it makes you feel.

Going forward there will be a specific example used describing a situation or decision to be made. This will be done to help show relationships between different ideas. When reading, please consider the relationships between ideas can be used in many different categories of life: Health, Wealth, Status, Confidence, Emotional well-being, Sociability, Character, Knowledge, Skill/Abilities, Family, Profession, Food, Sex, Clothing, Possessions, Dwelling/Residence, Life-preservation, Money, Power, Love, Romance, Happiness, Physical, Mental, Behavior, other.

It's encouraged to think about how ideas in this book could be applied to different categories of life- the ideas in this book are applicable in all these categories.

A. The Truth & representation of the truth

SO, ON THIS voyage of being a human being, and of human behavior the first topic that will be discussed is "The Truth". This is about the personality that you have developed. The personality you have developed consists of how you naturally act without thinking about it. And how that personality exists in the world right now, day-by-day, moment-by-moment.

The Truth can also be described as the actual intention a person has when taking a specific action. Somewhere between being conditioned by the environment and deciding goals that will influence the environment around you, your mind-spirit has developed an intention of the desired outcome of events. That intention is the only real truth that can be determined. What happens in the environment is anyones guess- did something happen for a good reason? Did something happen for a bad reason? Good or bad for who?

This concept of intention and truth is the basic foundation of understanding peoples actions in different situations. Day to day, conscious or unconscious, we all have different intentions. And how those intentions turn into the actions that our bodies produce in our environment, ends up being the representation of our intentions.

Our body lets us know about our environment and events happening in our environment and our mind-spirit may have arrived at a desire to see events play out a certain way (intention).

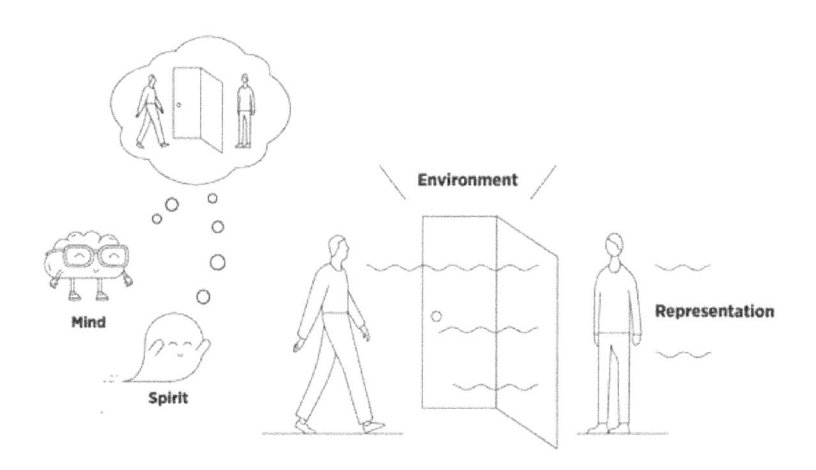

For example, being at work all day is a type of environment and through some time, a desire might develop to be at home (to rest or see family). Or a desire might develop to work more hours (for money or experience). Or a desire might develop to work fewer hours while gaining more. A desire develops, and then an intention takes hold. A desire to see future events unfold a certain way takes hold. The intention is how you want to the results of events to look like. It is imagining the future and seeing a completed event that has taken place.

If you intended to get to work early, something in the environment might have prevented you (and the actions you took) from doing so. Actions could of included setting your alarm clock to wake up earlier, taking a quicker route to work, skipping a morning ritual (like stopping at a store to get coffee/breakfast). Despite all intentions to get to work early, the environment prevented your intention to be completed. Events in the outside environment could of included a faulty alarm that did not make noise when it was set to, the quicker route to work might of had an accident causing delays. Anything in the environment could of prevented you from completing your intention to be at work early.

Your morning routine would look different to different people. People at work would see you did not arrive early. People who see you at a normal time on your commute would of noticed you were not there (coffee/breakfast person would of not seen you since you skipped their shop to save time). Neighbors you normally see at a certain time in their morning-pajamas would of noticed you are dressed for work instead of in your normal morning-pajamas. These people might make educated-guesses as to why there's a difference, but none of these people would know why unless it was communicated to them.

The various people you interact with in the environment would have developed a Perception of what has happened. Their Perception of what has happened includes any background knowledge of you, background knowledge of events, and the actions you took that are observable to them.

With you walking in the door at the normal time (not early), the only understanding co-workers might have is you did not arrive early, and you showed up at your normal time. Prior knowledge of your character, will influence their current Perspective as to why you were not early. People choose certain actions because it is believed it will benefit them. Actions are chosen over other actions because there is a belief it will be the best choice to benefit them best.

Communication with people in the environment about the actions you took will be a Representation of your actions. There will be the Perception of your actions other people have, and peoples Perception of your Representation. A

10 A. Truth and Representation of the Truth

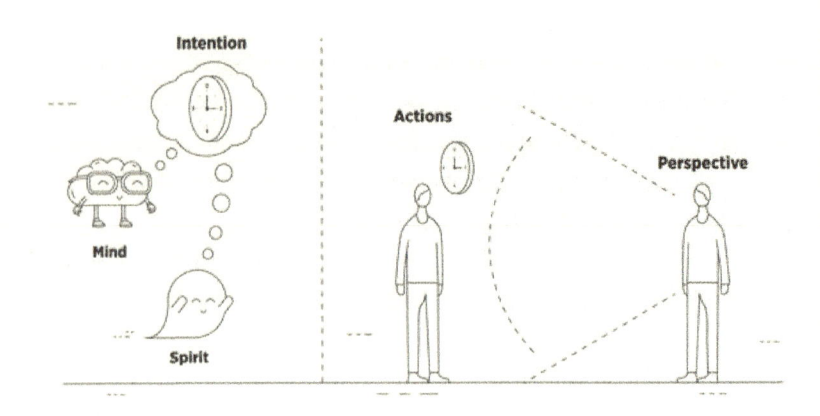

Representation of your actions is when there is an opportunity to communicate explaining your actions. It combines peoples Perception of your actions, with peoples Perception of your Representation (you explaining why you did what you did).

Explaining the actions you took (that aren't perceivable by your coworkers) such as setting your alarm earlier, taking a quicker route to work, and even skipping out on coffee/breakfast to get to work early will affect the Perception your coworkers will have. The communication you provide to actions you take represents you. The actions you take with no explanation also represents you.

With our good friend, coffee/breakfast person. With no prior communication of skipping the shop to arrive to work earlier, the coffee/breakfast person is very confused. Any number of situations could of happened of why you did not visit the shop that morning. Skipped breakfast,

Be: Common Sense for Uncommon People   11

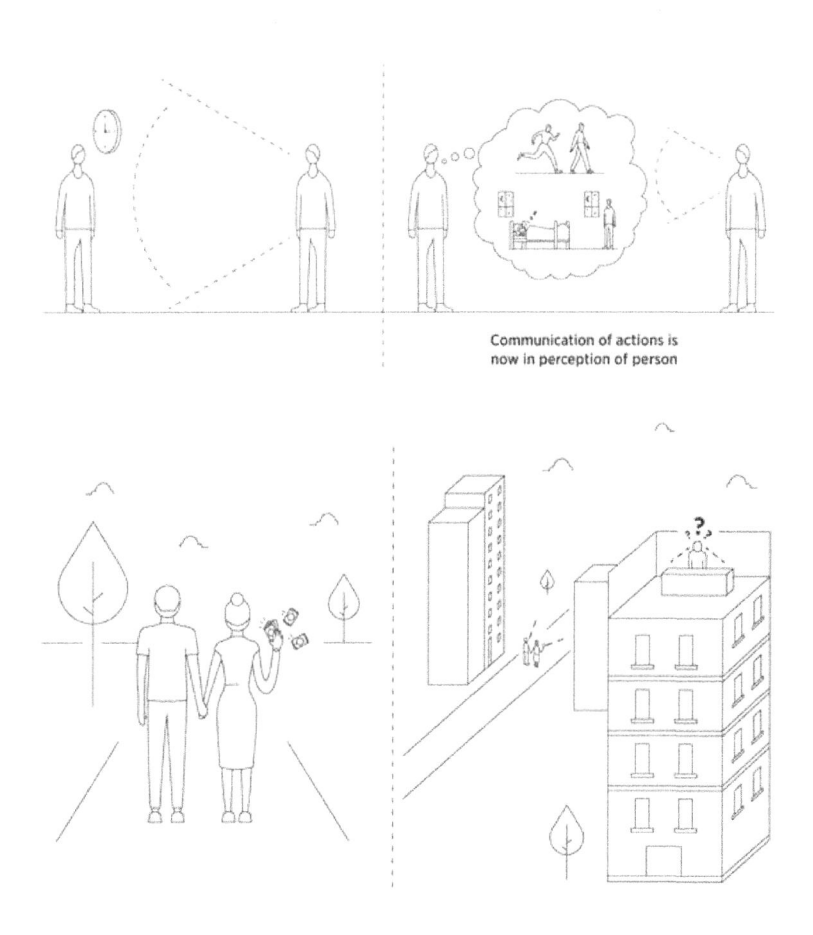

Communication of actions is
now in perception of person

got breakfast somewhere else and didn't need a second one, heaven-forbid you were in an accident and physically couldn't make it in for breakfast, hopefully had good fortune and were sidetracked by free stacks of money or heart-throbbing conversation with a new romantic interest. The Perception of breakfast-shop-person is only guesswork.

B. Forever smaller perspective and forever larger perspective

PERSPECTIVE ALSO TRANSLATES over to self-perception. Judging if you do or do not have something. If you are or are not satisfied in a category in life.

Unsatisfied Sad Have not No [Category]
Yes have happy Satisfied

Small list of various categories in life: Health, Wealth, Status, Confidence, Emotional well-being, Sociability, Character, Knowledge, Skill/Abilities, Family, Profession, Food, Sex, Clothing, Possessions, Dwelling/Residence, Life-preservation, Money, Power, Love, Romance, Happiness, Physical, Mental, Behavior, other You have a Perspective and are able to determine if you are a have or have not in a category in life. You also are able to determine if an idea (yours or otherwise) is a yes or a no. If something is a good idea or a bad idea. This is a closed decision. There is an absolute decision that will land on one side or another.

Outside of closed-decisions, there are degrees and types of decisions. There are multi-step decisions. There are degrees of quality to determine. If you do own an item, what quality is it? Is it the best of its kind? Is it fully functional or breaking-down? If making a decision is time a factor? Is it an absolute no, or just no for right now? Maybe later? Is it a "yes" for later?

A closed-decision process has an absolute answer, a yes or a no. Expanding on the yes or no, might involve quality. With everything you know about a category what is the best? What is the worst of it?

Worst------------------------[Category]------------------------Best

Small list of various category in life: Health, Wealth, Status, Confidence, Emotional well-being, Sociability, Character, Knowledge, Skill/Abilities, Family, Profession, Food, Sex, Clothing, Possessions, Dwelling/Residence, Life-preservation, Money, Power, Love, Romance, Happiness, Physical, Mental, Behavior, other Everything that you know about a category comes from yourself and the outside environment.

B. Forever Smaller Perspective and Forever Larger Perspective

Categories include physical possessions, people, feelings, various degrees of status, ideas, various situations, various lifestyles.

If you were able to make a list of things for a category there would be the Best and the Worst. On that list would be things that are not the best, but are good. Things that are not the Worst but are bad.

Worst-------Bad----------[Category]--------Good----------Best

List can include physical possessions, people, ideas, various situations, and of course- various categories in life (Small list of various categories in life: Health, Wealth, Status, Confidence, Emotional well-being, Sociability, Character, Knowledge, Skill/Abilities, Family, Profession, Food, Sex, Clothing, Possessions, Dwelling/Residence, Life-preservation, Money, Power, Love, Romance, Happiness, Physical, Mental, Behavior, other).

There would be various stages between the Best and the Worst. Various ways to describe the quality of a Category

Worst----Miserable-Bad--Unpleasant--[Category]---Pleasant----Good-Excellent--Best

Or even just on a out of 10 scale:

-10 -9 -8 -7 -6 -5 -4 -3 -2 -1 Category 1 2 3 4 5 6 7 8 9 10

Giving these notches definitions, allows you to determine exactly where something is on a Worst to Best scale. Creating a scale like this allows you to determine what is better than something else. It gives you a rating system based off your own knowledge and experiences of how you can classify things.

Knowledge and experience is limited though. A Best to Worst scale is temporary. There is always better and there is always worse. There are always additional ways to judge characteristics and always more notches that can be made.

Worse-------Worst------[Category]--------Best ---- Better

Even worse------Worse-------Worst------[Things]--------Best ---- Better----- Even better

-15 -14 -13 -12 -11 -10 -9 -8 -7 -6 -5 -4 -3 -2 -1 Things 1 2 3 4 5 6 7 8 9 10 11 12 13 14 15

-50 -40 -30 -20 -10 Things 10 20 30 40 50

Looking at various types of scales could include:

Broken not working kind of working working fully functional

Late delayed on time early

16   B. Forever Smaller Perspective and
      Forever Larger Perspective

depressed sad happy blissful

low Energy moderate energy high energy different same repetitive

Looking at your own life can look like a giant web of scales. A huge cross section of scales

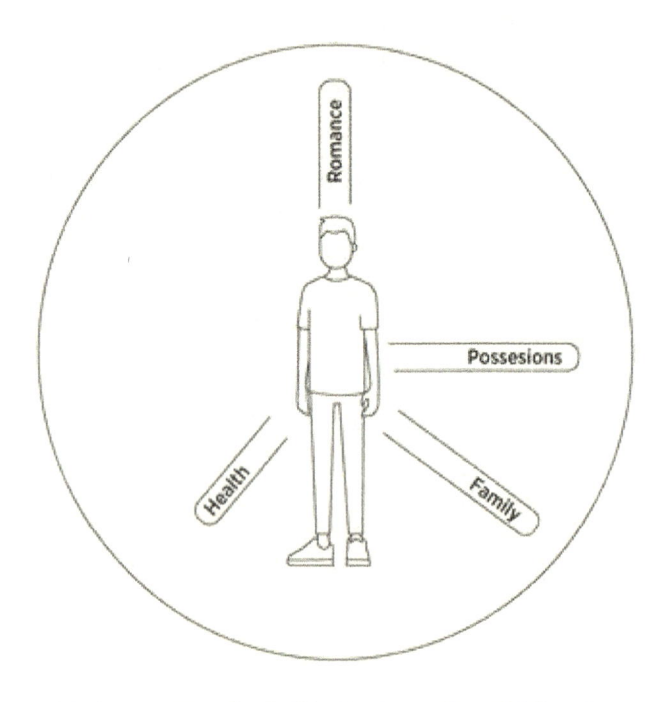

Various categories in life. You're at the middle of it.

C. Direction and focus with positive steps

WITH LITERALLY AN infinite number of categories that you can rate, there is a limited amount of time and attention you can give to each one. One of these categories could be skill-building. You know you can learn the finer points of of a skill as simple as folding paper planes / origami, the finer points of dry cleaning, or Advanced Thermodynamics, or anything. You can always excel at the skills that you have. However, most skills that are out there to learn or do, do not really matter to you. Generally, people focus on only a few aspects in their life and the skills behind those aspects that will benefit them the most. Any person can do anything, but not everything. There is only a limited amount of time to do things.

C. Direction and focus with positive steps

So, with so many choice and options of what you can do- how do you decide what to start on? Or continue on?

The reason why we choose an action (learning a skill, buying a certain type of car/clothing/jewelry/book, speaking to one person over another person, choosing one job over another job, taking a left turn instead of a right turn) is the perceived benefit choosing that action will give us. The perceived benefit of doing something is how we understand our environment will react to the action we take.

We may choose an action hoping for certain benefits to us. We may accomplish that action (become a master at a skill, buy the desired item, develop a relationship with a certain person, get a desired job) but after accomplishing that action- we may find the results are not what we hoped for. Hopefully accomplishing the goal, leads to all that was hoped for and more, sometimes not. This is where listening to your own intuition and feelings come in.

All the intelligence and knowledge in the world will still have blind spots and unintended outcomes. This is from perceiving how the environment of the world will react to an action we take and how the action we take will affect the environment of the world.

It's great to set goals and go after them is the point I'm trying to make. With the understanding, the main reason setting goals and accomplishing goals is even an understood thing in life- is that setting and accomplishing goals makes each of us feel a certain way doing it and after accomplishing it.

Negative	Positive
Sad	Happy
Shame	Pride
Insecure	Confident
Frustration	Excitement
Hate	Love
Disappointment	Satisfaction
Pain	Pleasure

If we set a goal, and along the way of accomplishing it we feel negative feelings, you need to remember to be flexible. Negative feelings is your body telling you a certain chosen plan of action is not working completely right. This is your body or intuition telling you there are possible blind spots or unintended outcomes behind corners you can't see that do not matchup with what you want your resulting benefits to be. This means the goal you decided on, may not give you the ending benefits you want. If you want to learn to fly to feel freedom, but getting in a plane and learning the controls is making you feel restricted and negative, the freedom you want to feel may be in another

C. Direction and focus with positive steps

goal and not in the sky. Picking up on these negative feelings tell you the way you are going about things, is not productive. More on how to pick the correct goal, in "Focus" below.

It is important to recognize these feelings. The are your unseen guideposts giving you direction in life. Absolutely on the same idea- when accomplishing an action- if you feel positive feelings, and you are really enjoying and having fun doing what you are doing- this is a good indication you are getting closer to your desired benefits. In alot of circumstances- especially around changing events, you may not have very strong feelings- positive or negative. Just understand the feelings are there. Change can be difficult. It usually is not all positive or all negative, but a little bit of each, slowly building up until traction is gained.

Focus
A new decision for a new goal will generally begin slowly. Over your current day it may just start as a perspective of what's going on around you, and noticing something in your day you only unconsciously notice, may plant a seed in you. Over some time, an idea or feeling may generate within you, leading you to start to feel something should be changed or different in your environment.

When you make the choice for a change to happen, this is one choice among other choices you make in your day. This choice can be very long term (change the world) or very short term (don't add hot sauce to your food). Something very important to the change taking place, in addition to listening to your positive and negative feelings- is how much you can focus on your goal.

When you have this idea for a change to happen, be specific about it! The more specific you are about your goal, the easier it will be for those guiding feelings to take place. Hopefully, those positive guiding feelings to tell you, you are on track. Having a goal that you know the resulting benefits of- will enable you to be more aware of opportunities to achieve that goal. *Opportunities* will start to <u>stand out</u> to you as if they have a **giant highlight** in real life. Without being specific about a goal, and being specific about the benefits you want to see from achieving that goal- your feelings will be less strong about it, and it will be more difficult to tell if you are achieving it, and also if you are closer to getting the resulting benefits.

How to be specific about goals
Once you decide on a goal, with the knowledge you decided on the goal with the best of intentions to benefit your life in a certain way- the most important thing to do from that point, will be to focus on how your life will be different once you accomplished your goal.

Take the time to sit down and really think about this. Goals don't all need to be challenges, they can be fun, seamless,

C. Direction and focus with positive steps

and easy. Sit down, or do whatever it is you need to do to understand once you accomplish your goal what will that change about your life? What positive benefits will accomplishing this goal bring to your life? Will that change your life on a day to day level? How will your life look different once you accomplished your goal? Once you accomplished your chosen goal, and this accomplishment is in your past- what will you do with your new life?

Cutting out harmful ingredients from your diet can give you new health and more energy. This would let you have more time to spend with people you want to spend it with and doing things you want to do- instead of worrying about health. With less time of negative health affecting you, you can use that free time to pursue other goals in life you would enjoy. Or really, that could be it- and just relax enjoying your newfound health. This could affect the size of clothes you buy, your medical expenses, your food choices. It could affect your friends if you choose to cut out certain ingredients/products/food/drink from your diet. You may find new friends or take space away from old ones. New friends could lead you to new places. New places to new situations. New choices. But these potential new changes are after you successfully cut out harmful ingredients from you diet.

The point of thinking about this, is to really make-solid in your mind that your goal will be accomplished. And different ideas of how your life can and will be different after accomplishing your goal.

The idea of the accomplishment goal in your mind- will let your mind think it's already done. The idea of the accomplished goal in your mind- will let you pick up opportunities through the day that will help you accomplish your goal.

Anything
Like with the ever possible mastery of any skill, there is the ever possibility of lifestyles. There are so many different types of lifestyles in your home maybe, in your neighborhood, or city or state. Or country, or hemisphere. Or last, so many lifestyles in the world we live in. Just so unbelievably many. The world is a small place, but we certainly fill it up with variety depending on where you look.

This is really important to know, or realize right now- because anything you want to do or see or hear or feel- there's a very strong chance you can find a group of like-minded folks already doing it. This means you already have support for what you believe in and want to do. It's there and happening right now. With goals and decisions and choices you can make, it's just up to you which lifestyle you want to live in. Once you make this decision for a goal or broader lifestyle you want, understanding how your life will look once this is an accomplished goal, and

C. Direction and focus with positive steps

having the discipline to maintain focus on it, will be the best way for you to live the type of life you desire.

Maintaining focus. Be in the moment
That feeling you had- when you saw your life after your goal or lifestyle is accomplished- that's the feeling you want to continue to have and continue to feel. This will be good.

You want to support that feeling, and supporting that feeling will support the level and intensity of focus you will give to getting that goal/lifestyle.

What motivates you to continue? What do you enjoy? What around you bring out the positive feelings? What around you brings out those feelings you felt thinking about your new life once your goal is complete?

Many people have listed the following:

Pictures/photographs around them that when looking at them reminded them of the goal-new-life accomplished feeling, video/music that brought back the positive feelings, Having like-minded individuals around, Having a group to pursue the goal with, laying down closing their eyes and just mentally seeing the new lifestyle they want to live (getting deeper and deeper into details)

These are just some ideas. Whatever supports your positive feelings, or reignite those feelings of being in and living your new lifestyle/accomplished goal are things that are recommended to keep doing. This will maintain your focus. Fuel your ability to see opportunities. And get you to where you want to be that much sooner. Feel good!

D. Achieving a Goal

ALTHOUGH, ON THE way to accomplishing any possible chosen goal or lifestyle, there could be "barriers" that popup occasionally. All goals or lifestyle accomplishments might not always be immediately available to jump-into, not a "Step 1 --to→ goal" path but there might be little rest-stops along the way (think: Step 1--to-->Step 2--to→ goal).

The various steps that popup prior to reaching your set-goal is just that- steps. You moved forward, and if you're not at your goal yet, you need to take another step forward.

If it's that simple it great. Keep taking steps and life is easy. You'll step your way easily into your end-goal and be living wonderfully (more wonderfully).

| 1 | 2 | 3 | 4 | Goal |

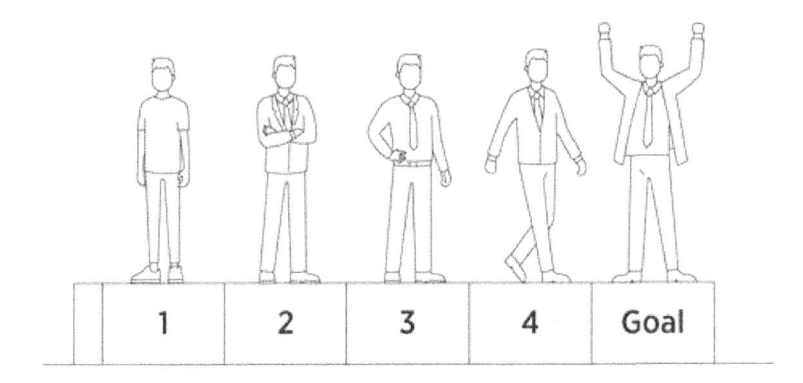

Obstacles

Taking steps forward and being able to accomplish your goal is great. That's lucky. If it's just as easy as moving forward. But, to reach your goal, you might need as some point to take a step up. Going from the first floor to the second floor of a building, you must first enter the building, take steps forward, then physically lift your leg AND move it forward to reach the first higher step that will lead you to the second floor.

To some, this is too much and got lost, or lost interest when I skipped the word "Elevator". That's fine, that is you listening to your body and understanding you have limits on what you can or choose to do.

For those that choose to battle on and forward, if that first step up and forward didn't have you reach your goal (the second floor), you need to keep stepping up and forward.

D. Achieving a Goal

Strength / Determination / Ability
Simply said: you can lose strength during the process of reaching your goal. You can take a break regain strength and continue the process. Not all gains can always be done quickly in one step and generally astronomical-gains is an incremental process (many steps) and not done in one small-quick step.

If you lose strength or motivation or determination, this is where you support systems come into play. You can either regain strength on your own. You can use your support systems (from the prior chapter, we learned support systems are things that encourage you to keep going, to feel the feelings of already having what you want, and just imagining yourself in that moment). Support systems can include material objects, thoughts, meditation, video/movies/photos/music, friends, family, anything you can put in front of you to gain strength, gain determination and gain motivation to keep going.

Taking a break and gaining back your strength, you're now continuing the process of acquiring your goal! This is great. This is an ability onto itself. Having the ability to stay motivated, and the ability to stay determined, and the ability to stay happy while pursuing your goal is one ability that many people seek to have. Everyone has it, but to different degrees. This ability like any other is an ability that just improves with time as you practice it.

In addition to this ability you have to keep-going-moving-forward-making-progress, an ability that is necessary is to determine what steps are ahead of you.

Trying to get to the second floor of the building from the first floor- are all the steps up equal in size? Do you need to step higher on certain steps than others? Are there any cracks in the stairs you need to watch out for? Are there any spills you should avoid? Are there people walking down or up? What type of obstacles are in front of you?

These are easy. These are easy obstacles. You just need to look at what is in front of you, and have an idea of what you need to do to take the first movement towards your goal. Then take the first movement!

Tougher obstacles will appear, more challenging ones. Obstacles that do not move, that are not tricking you, obstacles that are your friend, these are just opportunities. These things in your path is just you deciding how

D. Achieving a Goal

you want to reach your goal. Next, we will look into when obstacles or barriers come up that are in conflict with you. That do not want you to get what you want, or want a different outcome than you want. Obstacles that you have a general idea of- are easy, these are good opportunities. These type of obstacles are your friend. They are only a roadmap, you get to choose how to get to where you want to go.

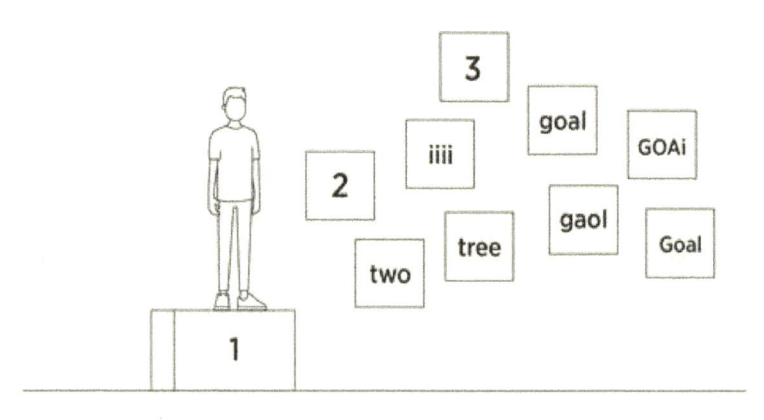

E. Understanding Obstacles

Changing Obstacles

OBSTACLES MAY NOT always be as obvious as immediately knowing how to solve or get past it. As soon as you come in front of a door, you know you can open it to "conquer" the obstacle. If you find an object is in front of you blocking your path from walking forward, you know you can step over it, step around it, move it- to continue forward.

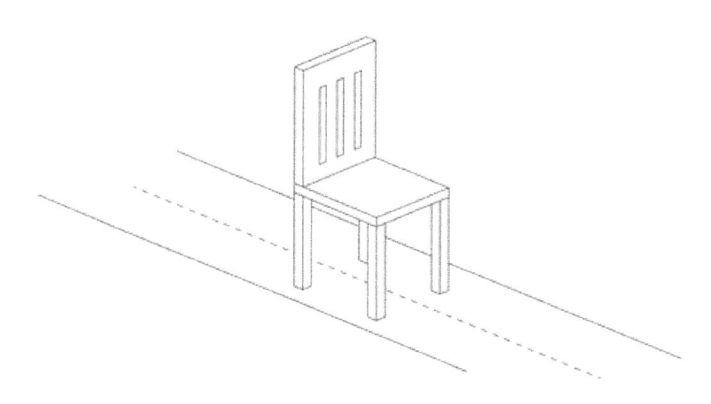

E. Understanding Obstacles

There are other obstacles that aren't as obvious as physical ones that popup. The first being your own perception of obstacles. If you view a chair in front of you that is blocking your path from continuing forward, you might think you could step around it, and you might be right, but you decide to move it instead. You discover the chair is bolted to the ground.

The chair cannot be moved (at least not-easily, lifting it with your hands and moving it aside is not an option). So, your perception was that this was a normal chair, that could be easily picked up and moved but discovered it could not be moved. Why? You tried to lift it and discovered it couldn't be lifted, maybe it was heavier than you thought? Try again to do the same thing but with more strength in lifting- same result. Look at the chair and see what it could possibly be- you discover it's legs are bolted to the ground. Ok, so you know you can get tools and remove the bolts and then move the chair, but those tools are not immediately accessible, and it's much more work than necessary to reach your goal. You thought there was an obstacle in your way, and you were correct in this perspective. But, did not perceive the obstacle correctly. Through trial and error and observation you discovered the obstacle was more complex than you originally thought. You accurately found out "The Truth" of the environment (the real situation) behind the obstacle (it wasn't just in your way and easily movable, it was in your way and NOT easily moveable) and then applied the correct step to overcome the obstacle (you stepped around it and moved forward).

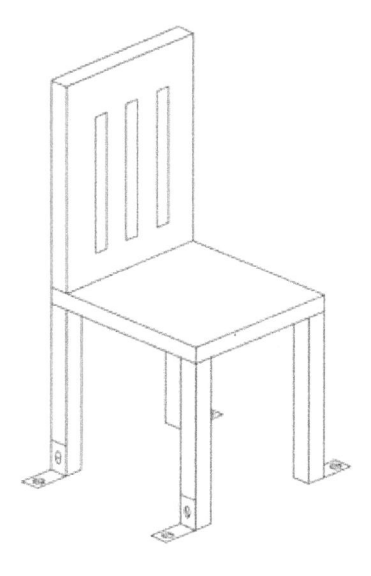

In this example, we learned (or knew already) that we have to first do our best with what we know. When what we know proved not to be true, we determined what is The Truth of things before us. This allowed us to attempt a new solution to the problem at-hand. We attempted the new solution, and the solution worked (stepping aside and moving forward).

There are no things such as simple problems or tough ones, just situations. The situations can resolve themself in many ways.

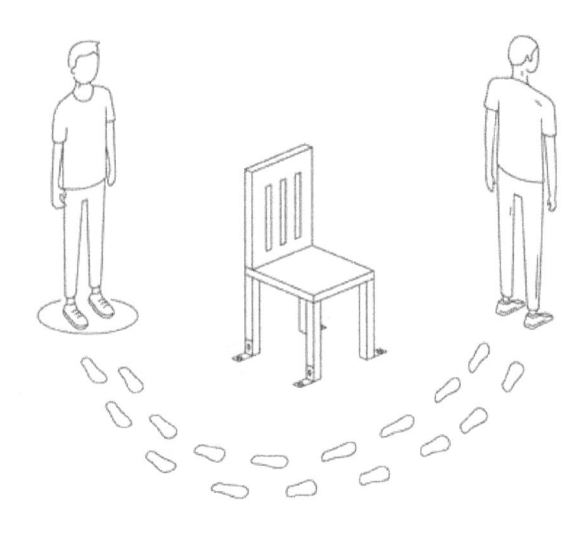

People

The mighty chair. The mighty chair and all it's bolts could not stop us. Neither will this person sitting in that chair. And first, why would they want to stop us? That person in the chair is our friend. Friends want each other to be successful.

While friends wish the best for one another, just like our perspective on what's going on around us (we can't know everything), they unfortunately can't know everything either.

The friend in that chair may be sitting down and facing the opposite direction as you try to pass their chair (in this case- you noticed a person sitting in that chair, and are NOT trying to lift the chair with the person sitting in it, but immediately decide to walk around the person sitting in the chair).

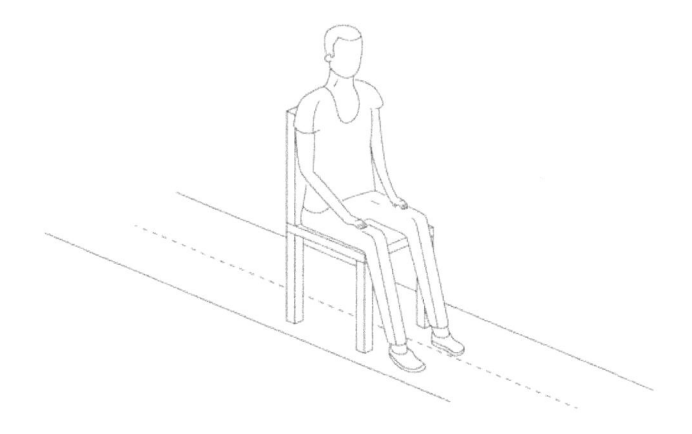

So, as you step to the side and continue walking forward, you successfully accomplish moving forward past that obstacle. As you're looking forward to your next destination- you feel pressure on your right arm, and it intensifies, it intensifies to the side of your chest and body- what's happening? The person sitting in the chair has bumped into you. As you were concentrating on your next objective, so were they. They did not see you walking and have bumped into you.

This of course, takes you slightly off course- as it is a time delay, and although very light and friendly, the bump

36   E. Understanding Obstacles

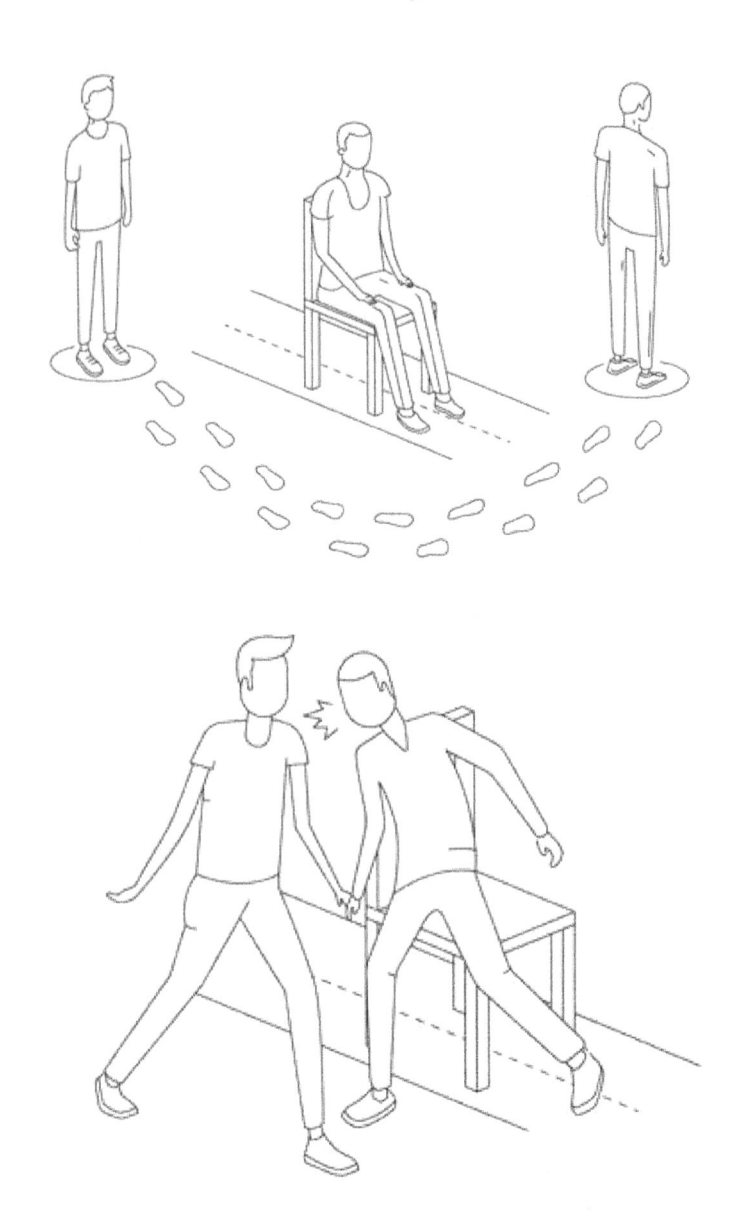

distracts you slightly and you have to regain your composure (figure out what happened, figure out what is happening, then figure out what to do next). In this case, you two give each other a head nod in understanding this was unintentional and you both proceed onto your destinations.

A coincidence. An unrelated event happened that through no fault on your own, or intention of another occured. That's all that happened. What that meant for you (and that person) is the bump (caused by the unintentional walking into each other) delayed you both momentarily before you could both regain composure and continue on your goal.

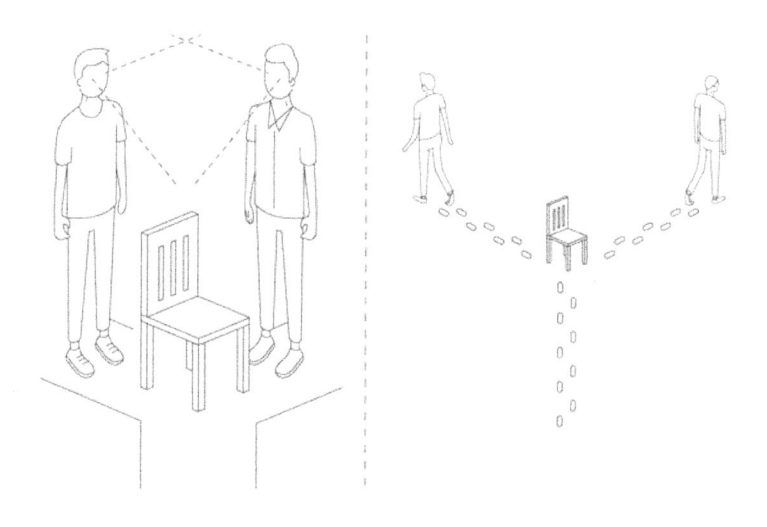

More on people

Such a great story so far, let's continue! Summary: As, you see the chair with your friend on it looking the opposite way, you sidestep this obstacle in your way, and walk forward, happy to be moving forward with your goal- until the bump comes into place, but thankfully you both nod and continue on your way. Continuing: As you continue on your way, that same person right after bumping, nodding, and continuing, runs back to you. The nod apparently was not sufficient enough. The person wants to speak with you and express guilt for accidentally bumping into you. Which is well enough, they could of come back to chat, talk, give you an item, ask for an item, or anything.

The point is, while on your way to do what you want to do, to reach your goal, there is a person here chatting with you. The only goal on your mind, your only intention is to keep moving forward to reach your goal. Despite all of the persons good-intentions of wanting a good relationship with you (thus running back to you to apologize) they negatively affect you. They are lacking the perception (and understanding) that you only want to continue forward. Occasionally, good intentions of an individual will not be easily understood if those good intentions are negatively affecting you.

The easy solution to this is to explain to the person your intentions- of desiring only to move forward, no more additional time is necessary to address the bump. This is you taking action to explain your intentions (of wanting to move forward). The words you use to explain the situation to the other person is your Representation. The tone, body language, words chosen, are the actions you are taking to express your intentions, the total event of your explanation to the other person is the Representation of your actions (of your intention).

The other person will hear the words you say and interpret those words. The way they perceive what and how you say, is their Perception of events. It's their Perception of your Representation. If all went well, you found a problem (something that negatively affects you, in this case: the person taking up additional time of yours) and you also found a solution to this problem (verbally explaining

E. Understanding Obstacles

to the person additional time speaking about the bump is not necessary, you want to continue forward to your next destination). With people, and any issues that come up is about doing your best to Perceive the situation correctly, and applying the correct action to solve the situation. With any luck, the situation will seamlessly and easily be solved with the first action you take to solve the situation.

More on solving this type of situation in Section G.

Changing Barriers - People
Occasionally, situations will not be solved on a first attempt. This is where your Inner Strength, Determination, and Ability to continue come in. What just happened is after that

bump took place, there was a chat. The chat was an issue. You identified an issue, and did your best to solve it. You took Action (verbally communicated with the other person: the chat was not necessary).

In the ideal scenario, the person Perceived your actions as well-intentioned, wanting only both of you to have success in what you were doing and where you were going, understood that (and understood your desire of wanting to continue forward to your next destination) and your actions achieved the goal of letting you move forward.

But in this case, despite your Intentions, your actions were Perceived negatively by the other person. In the Action you took, it could of been tone, body language, something in the background that temporarily distracted that person from what you were saying- and in affect missed something important. The person Perceived your well-meaning dialog negatively. They took an Action (going back to you to chat) they felt best represented their Intention (of making sure the relationship was still in good health after the bump) and they Perceived your Action (of explaining you want to continue to your destination and not spend additional-time chatting) negatively.

Very determined to keep a healthy relationship between the two of you, the other person wanted to continue to chat, and spend additional time chatting. They might have

E. Understanding Obstacles

thought if you do not want to spend additional-time chatting, then clearly the bump affected the relationship very negatively (even though it did not, you just want to do your thing and move forward to your next destination). The additional-time chatting negatively affects you and your goals, while only good-intentions is on the part of the other person (and yourself) in wanting to keep a healthy relationship (and for you- continue forward to your next destination).

After your first attempt to solve the situation did not work, you tried again. You did not do much different, only maybe spoke higher (to overcome background noise), spoke more clearly and slowly (to make sure your words could be clearly understood), and maybe added on an additional sentence or two to explain that the relationship was healthy between you two, and an additional sentence or two to explain your desire and focus is not concerned with the bump or the health of the relationship, but only with moving towards your next destination and understanding the person has a destination to go to as well.

After the first attempt to explain your desire to move forward failed, you took another look at the situation. Seems like you explained yourself clearly the first time that would allow you to "win" by continuing onto your next destination, and also for your friend (the other person) to "win" by addressing their concern of the relationship still being healthy and to continue on with progress towards his/her next destination. With everything being a win scenario for everyone involved, you are confused as to why your friend (the other person), why he or she is not accepting of your explanation.

Whenever someone gets what they want, that should let the situation continue forward. But your friend, he or she wanted to keep chatting. By your Perspective, you can only determine their needs have not been fully met- the Representation they put forward of continuing to chat can only lead you think you did not properly address their needs.

E. Understanding Obstacles

The wonderful thing about the relationship between Intention and Actions is that there is a delay. From taking Action yourself, or Perceiving the Action others take, is there is a delay for that to be processed. Your friend may of completely Perceived your Action but it took time for their own feelings of comfort and acceptance of the situation to be Represented in their own actions. So even though your friend, he or she after your first attempt, wanted to continue the conversation, this doesn't mean you necessarily failed after your first attempt. Only it took that person an extra moment to accept what you were saying (gaining the feeling for comfort/acceptance with what you said)- you might of done something different in your second attempt to explain how you would "win" (by continuing onto your next destination), and how they would "win" (by addressing their need of making sure the relationship was in good health), but what changed was the time that passed by- which was enough time for them to accept was you said the first time (to feel comfortable that they did "win"; to feel they accomplished what they needed to in the chat- making sure the relationship is still in good health after the very unfortunate bump that took place).

Just as easily though, they might not of Perceived everything your Intention to put forward in your Actions that would show they would "win" in the situation (just as much as you would "win" in the situation). They might of understood they would "win" but missed how you would "win" -- and wanting to keep the relationship healthy, wanted to make sure they were not being Perceived negatively because of their lack of concern for you "winning" (you gaining satisfaction in accomplishing your goals) and continued the chat with the new Intention of verifying that you would also accomplish your goals.

What's going on in this type of situation is that there is an issue or problem. There is a solution attempted. The solution will work or it will not work. The way solutions work is by satisfying main concerns of the problem. The first solution may work, but it may take time for that solution to be accepted. The solution may work for some parts of the problem, but not all parts of the problem. That means the problem is still there. It may take more time to develop a new Perspective of the problem. Gaining a new Perspective allows you see different parts of the problem. This will allow you to address those new parts of the problem. Addressing those newly-seen parts might mean you have fully addressed the problem. Once all parts of a problem are addressed- that's a Win.

In some situations, not all parts of a problem have to be addressed to continue forward to your next destination. Which is still a Win. Enough parts of the problem have been addressed to have comfort and acceptance in you moving forward to your next destination. The problem was not fully resolved, but partially. In some situations, a partial solution is all that is needed for a Win. Situations where everyone gains enough comfort and acceptance of a solution to a problem is a called a Win-Win situation.

Win-Win situations allow the greatest momentum to progress toward your goals and next destination.

F. Win-Win

THERE ARE MANY different types of solutions. A solution is ultimately finding the answer to a situation. There are many answers to the same question.

Sometimes, the answer to a question or a solution to a problem can leave some people dissatisfied. This is unfortunate. It is unfortunate for the person or people that feel dissatisfied. The answer to the question or solution to a problem came from somewhere. Either through the decision of one person of the agreement of many.

As described earlier, dissatisfaction or having different/conflicting goals with a person (where you want your goal, and the other person wants their goal, and you both are just focused on getting to your goal, not helping or hurting the other persons goal) can happen. A decision maker can be trying to get to their goal and may be paying no mind to the dissatisfied people. The people that were dissatisfied with an answer or solution may not of had enough influence in a situation.

For something to happen, there has to be enough agreement that it should happen. For a decision-maker that is after a "win" (a "win" is them reaching their goal), they need to win over enough parts of a problem or question to make the answer "Pass". Some decisions are simply Pass or Fail. Many intensely focused on getting to their destination (their goal) many address only enough parts of a question or problem to get enough "winning" answers or enough winning "solutions" so that way any bump (conflict/dilemma) becomes a "Pass" and they can continue forward.

And that's fine- to be so focused as to want to consistently, and constantly be moving forward towards the end-goal. The only issue that comes up is with the left-behind portions of the answer/solution that have not been addressed.

And to summarize a prior point, the left-behind portions of an answer/solution were left behind because of a decision-makers focus on moving forward. The decision-maker is only able to move forward because enough parts of a solution has made it allowable for him or her to continue moving forward. Having enough parts of a answer allowing someone to move forward means on at least the decision-makers behalf- best-intentions were involved in the decision making process. Best intentions have to be involved in the decision making process because nothing can move forward if there isn't enough momentum behind a decision to allow it to move forward. -- Back to the bump: after explaining the second time around, this addressed any additional issues that needed resolving and also took into account the time-delay of acceptance the person might need to have their actions reflect their Perspective.

Moving forward, back to the left-behind portions of the answer/solution. The decision-maker was very focused to continue moving forward to their next destination/end-goal. And more power to them. Good for them, and good luck. However, in their rush to move forward, there were un-addressed portions of a situation that needed acceptance/solution/answer. When the decision-maker makes it to the destination/end-goal, those left-behind parts of that question/situation will still be there. This means when the decision-maker is at their next destination or accomplished their original goal, those left-behind parts from that prior bump will still want satisfaction.

Leaving behind unfulfilled portions of a situation happens in every situation. Just like not being able to Perceive or know everything that goes on- this trickles down to leaving parts of a situation left-behind. -- When they said they just wanted to move forward and the relationship was healthy I saw their eyebrow lift, did they mean it? When I said I just wanted to move forward and the relationship was healthy I felt my eyebrow lift up more than usual- did I need to explain that weird body movement? -- Something is always left behind in a situation. Not everything can be known, and not everything can be explained for- there would be explanation of explanations that explained things and nothing would ever get done and nobody would ever move forward, people would just sit around explaining things all day.

On one side of a scenario, we have things that are left-behind because it wasn't really relevant, or they were left-behind because those specific answers didn't have enough influence to prevent events from moving forward. Within the same scenario- of things being left-behind, is when things that are left-behind do still have a significant amount of influence to affect future progress towards a decision-makers goal.

When a decision-maker moves forward from a bump, or a scenario, or whatever the situation may be, and there is significant amounts of things left behind from a prior scenario, or maybe not alot- but the very few things or thing left behind carries very significant influence, this could affect the progress of the decision-makers ability to continue to their goal, it could affect the decision-makers ability to stay completed/accomplished/satisfied after achieving the goal, and after achieving it could affect the decision-makers ability to move onto future goals/destinations.

With addressing as many parts as possible, giving very good care to not leave relevant ideas or people left-behind in a situation has it's benefits. This means for the decision-maker progressing toward their goal, staying satisfied in the accomplishment of their goal, and moving forward towards future goals will have much less chance of resistance. Acknowledging as many parts of a situation as possible means those parts are supporting you now. Acknowledging and satisfactorily answering parts of a question/situation/problem means these are things that support you onto your goal, these are things that support you as you achieve your goal, and these are things that support you as you move towards your next goal. Acknowledging and satisfactorily completing relevant parts of a situation allow you to build momentum as you have more support from prior bumps, you have more support from prior situations/issues/events that will not hinder you but help you.

G. Win-Win now, Win-Win later

WHEN CREATING SOLUTIONS, or taking steps forward, there is already a degree of creativity involved. Deciding how to take a step forward, resolve a situation, in which style takes creativity, along with the pace of moving forward, and deciding how much relevant things from a prior situation should be satisfied before moving forward.

Generally, if there is a very tough situation where the steps forward is a thin decision- there is heavy support for one decision and heavy resistance (but more support than resistance) for another decision- absolutely, you're able to move forward. It's likely that heavy resistance to moving forward will affect you as you progress towards your new destination, and it is likely it will affect you as you reach your destination, and as you continue to progress toward other destinations/goals.

There's a few ways to address that type of situation. Creativity will be the way out of tough situations. Something behind the wants and needs of both sides will be able to be satisfied by a resolution neither decision is currently allowing. This could be a difference of time for something to happen, a style of something happening, or the fact that something will happen at all (or other resistance/opposition). It'll be up to you to find out how fluid the situation is and what you can do with it to change opposition to support.

People oppose things because it will (seemingly) conflict with the way they determine their lifestyle allows. Allowing the input and expression of resistance or potential resistance helps you gain insight into what they would like their lifestyle to be. It allows insight into what their desired outcome is. Allowing expression allows you to understand how the resistance or potential resistance to a decision acts. Their action and words could be different. Their actions may show what their desired outcome really is. Alot of times, resistance or potential resistance will not be sure of what they want as an outcome. The "resistance" to a decision could just be undecided and not really care. Viewing actions allows you to see what resistance to a decision may enjoy seeing as an outcome.

The undecided to an outcome may look as resistance to a decision, but undecided may just be happy doing their own thing. If there isn't support for an idea, does not mean

G. Win-win now, Win-win Later

that it is resistance to an idea. While expressing yourself and trying to reach your own goal, it'll be important to understand who supports you, who is resisting your idea, and who doesn't really care either way. The group that is undecided, or doesn't really care- understanding that groups actions will never help nor harm your progress is a group that you can pass on by. It's a series of actions or decisions by the undecided that will neither help nor harm your cause. Focusing and bringing attention towards that group will distract from your progress towards your goal. Continue forward after deciding a group is undecided. They will be happy to continue doing whatever it is they are doing. You'll be happy to continue making progress towards your goal.

With a bunch of supporters with you moving forward, being able to have the peace of mind there are some undecided groups or instances you can easily pass by and not dedicate time or effort to- like a freebie, there will sometimes be resistance that you were not able to address and may still resist as you have enough support to keep making progress to your goal. Are satisfied after reaching your goal. Or are progressing toward new goals.

You took the time to understand the resistance or potential resistance. You took the time to have dialog with the resisting groups and understand any emotions and ideas that were expressed to have an idea of the type lifestyle these groups would want to have as a goal. This helps you determine what types of actions you can take to have the conflicting ideas between your goal and the resistance-goal can be made to change resisting actions to -if not supporting ones- as least actions that will not affect your progress.

So while progressing towards your goal, you made best efforts to ensure the most relevant groups that were not supporting you and were left-behind- their concerns and ideas were addressed (so anything resisting that was left-behind will not affect your progress in the future). But despite all your best efforts, there were still some areas you could not take care of- at least right then and there.

Not always relevant, but in some situations and circumstances, you'll be able to put a system in place to automatically address any future conflicting ideas with yours. Such as if a goal is weight loss, you can take a one-time action and eat a salad instead of french fries (eat something low-calories instead of something high-calories). That is a decision. Having something automatic in place to address future-conflicting ideas would be making a decision to develop a habit that in all future meals, you will always choose a low-calorie meal over a high-calorie meal. That would be something that would be automatically address future conflicts (in this case- the decision of what to eat). Another example would be something like becoming financially rich. But there is debt in place preventing you from moving forward with your plans to become financially-rich. An example of setting up an automatic system to address future-conflicts (in this case, the debt) would be to setup automatic payments to the debt. That way you address the conflict (the debt) automatically, and it does not take attention or focus away from your goal (becoming financially-rich). The resistance in this case was the debt.

Automatically addressing resisting ideas, or people will give you the opportunity to reduce any resistance towards your goal, allow to concentrate and move forward in progress towards your goal, and any resistance with something automatically addressing it will either be a non-issue or eventually turn resistance into support.

BONUS SECTION

Final thoughts
TAKE CARE OF yourself
Focus on yourself. People will focus on themselves. Sacrificing oneself for others exists but that love isn't for everybody, it's for very few people we care so much about to sacrifice ourselves for. So, focus on yourself. Other people will be there. There will be people there to help you. The people that are there to help you will be changing with time. All with different talents and abilities, people will come and go. Focus on building yourself to who you want you to be. The team you have around you now might or might not be there in the future for various reasons. When you get stronger, you can take better care of the ones around you that you care for. Members of your team will change as your needs change.

Body, Mind, Spirit
You can build your body, you can build your knowledge base and how smart you get, and you can build your spirit (your will power and your motivation).

Rent, Projects, Social
Pay your rent, make sure you have food clothing and shelter. Past that you can work on projects outside of the main way you maintain a lifestyle. These projects can be for fun or a new potential source of income. If you have any luck, it will be something fun that will be a new source of income. Social- in a lifestyle pursuing things for the sake of interest and fun, and not to further ones own goals is really necessary to a balanced life. Enjoying the company of others, pursuing friendships and social-happiness is an important part of a balanced lifestyle.

Goals, Appreciation
Pick a goal, don't limit yourself. Everything is possible, it's just a matter of if you can make the moves quick enough to get where you want to go before time is up. Reaching smaller goals are accomplishments, these are things to appreciate. Things can always be better or worse, very important to appreciate what you currently have. Goals are things you can work towards. Always do your best to maintain and appreciate what you currently have- life gives standards to nobody, what you have is a gift.

Priorities
There's going to be a balancing act of priorities. It's going to be on a scale that you choose for yourself on how to weigh different opportunities. You can do anything but not everything. To maintain what you have, there is going to be a minimum amount of attention you'll have to focus on it. As your goals and priorities change for the type of lifestyle you want, the amount of attention towards some of these opportunities in life can change. You have only a certain amount of attention you can give, there's only 24 hours in each day to dedicate time to. You'll have to decide which opportunities in life you need to give attention to, how much attention is necessary to maintain those opportunities in life, and what opportunities you want to give more attention to.

Like before- rent social projects, you'll need to maintain yourself (food clothing shelter) before you can grow socially and develop projects. Like before- mind body spirit, you'll need to maintain who you are before you can grow your mind, before you can grow your body, before you can grow your spirit. The requirements of life need you to take care of your current lifestyle, before you can start to switch it up, change it around, and really mix it up. Have a good foundation. From a good foundation you can plan the work you want to do then go out and work the plan.

Conclusion

THANK YOU FOR reading. I hope this was of some value to yourself or someone you know. If so, please keep this in mind for recommendation to others that might benefit from it.

If this has positive feedback of people enjoying this writing and would like to see more, I plan to write in more detail and/or on additional topics. If it does not, I plan to continue to do my best to be a contributing and supportive person to society and individuals in need.

If you'd like to reach out to me for dialog please send me an email at BeBookCSUP@gmail.com Writing this, there was alot of dialog from myself to others, and from others to myself. I'd like to continue that.

Conclusion

If able and willing, and want to support me and my future projects, good reviews and feedback is appreciated. Just talking about this book with others and letting them know of the benefit you found in it. Sending out a tweet, posting a good review, letting someone know. Lastly and unseen by me- just using it and the ideas in it to your benefit. The whole point in this book is the idea to make your life easier. I hope it has already and will again and more in the future. Please give back to others whenever possible. Best wishes!

Additional Resources

EVERYTHING LISTED BELOW are additional resources you could use if you are interested in learning more about various perspectives and lifestyle choices people decide to use. Each listing is a resource that can be absorbed to learn about a specific Section or as a jumping off point ("if you're interested in this resource, you may also be interested in...") to find similar resources that might better fit yourself.

Section | Description
- **A** Truth and Representation of the Truth
- **B** Forever smaller perspective and forever larger perspective
- **C** Direction and focus with positive steps
- **D** Achieving a Goal
- **E** Understanding Obstacles

F Win-Win
G Win-Win now, Win-Win later

[Section letter] Resource
Section letter listed means the resource is geared mainly for that Section.

No Section letter listed means it is all-englufing. Many topics in the resource will touch on all sections.

Below are Additional Resources, listed in categories, but no specific order

Reading
Written with more theory than story (the emphasis is on direct statements)

The 48 Laws of Power by Robert Greene (2000)
[A] The Selfish Gene by Richard Dawkins (2016)
Emotional Intelligence: Why It Can Matter More Than IQ by Daniel Goleman (2005)
Introducing NLP: Psychological Skills for Understanding and Influencing People (Neuro-Linguistic Programming) by Joseph O'Connor (1993)
[B, C, D] Who Moved My Cheese? by Spencer Johnson (2006)
The Mystery Method: How to Get Beautiful Women Into Bed by Mystery (2007)
The New Rules of Attraction: How to Get Him, Keep Him, and Make Him Beg for More by Arden Leigh (2011)

[A, B] The Art Of Seduction by Robert Greene (2004)

Written with more story than theory (the emphasis is on stories to show choices in action)

[A, B] A Brief History of Time by Stephen Hawking (1998)
Elon Musk: Tesla, SpaceX, and the Quest for a Fantastic Future by Ashlee Vance (2015)
I'm Feeling Lucky: The Confessions of Google Employee Number 59 by Douglas Edwards (2012)
Marissa Mayer and the Fight to Save Yahoo! by Nicholas Carlson (2016)
[A,B,C] Rules of the Game by Neil Strauss (2012)
[C,D,E] Brunelleschi's Dome: How a Renaissance Genius Reinvented Architecture by Ross King (2013)
[C,D,E] The Mystic Masseur by V. S. Naipaul (2002)
[D,E,F] The BillHow Legislation Really Becomes Law: A Case Study of the National Service Bill by Steven Waldman (1996)

Watchables
More theory than story (the emphasis is on direct statements)

[C] The Secret (2007)

More story than theory (the emphasis is on stories to show choices in action)

[A, B] Cosmos Carl Sagan (1980)
[D] Groundhog Day (1993)
[G] Interview (Forbes): JayZ and Warren Buffet on Success and Giving Back (2010)
[E] Office Space (1999)
[D] Ferris Bueller's Day Off (1986)
[D] Wonder Woman (2017)

Made in the USA
Coppell, TX
27 November 2021